Willy Can Count

By Anne Rockwell

Arcade Publishing · New York

Little, Brown and Company

First Edition

Library of Congress Catalog Card Number 89-83839
Library of Congress Cataloging-in-Publication Data is available.
ISBN 1-55970-013-0

Published in the United States
by Arcade Publishing, Inc., New York, a Little, Brown company

Published simultaneously in Canada
by Little, Brown & Company (Canada) Limited
Printed in the United States of America
Designed by Marc Cheshire

BP

1 3 5 7 9 10 8 6 4 2

Willy went walking
with his mother.
"I can count," he said.
"Good!" said Mother.
"What can you count?"

"I can count one brown cow,"
 said Willy.
"Good!" said Mother.
"What can you count two of?"

"I can count two red birds,"
said Willy.
"Good!" said Mother.
"What can you count three of?"

"I can count three yellow chicks,"
said Willy.
"Good!" said Mother.
"What can you count four of?"

"I can count four orange ladybugs,"
 said Willy.
"Good!" said Mother.
"What can you count five of?"

"I can count five pink pigs,"
said Willy.
"Good!" said Mother.
"What can you count six of?"

"I can count six green frogs,"
said Willy.
"Good!" said Mother.
"What can you count seven of?"

"I can count seven gray squirrels,"
said Willy.
"Good!" said Mother.
"What can you count eight of?"

"I can count eight blue moths,"
said Willy.

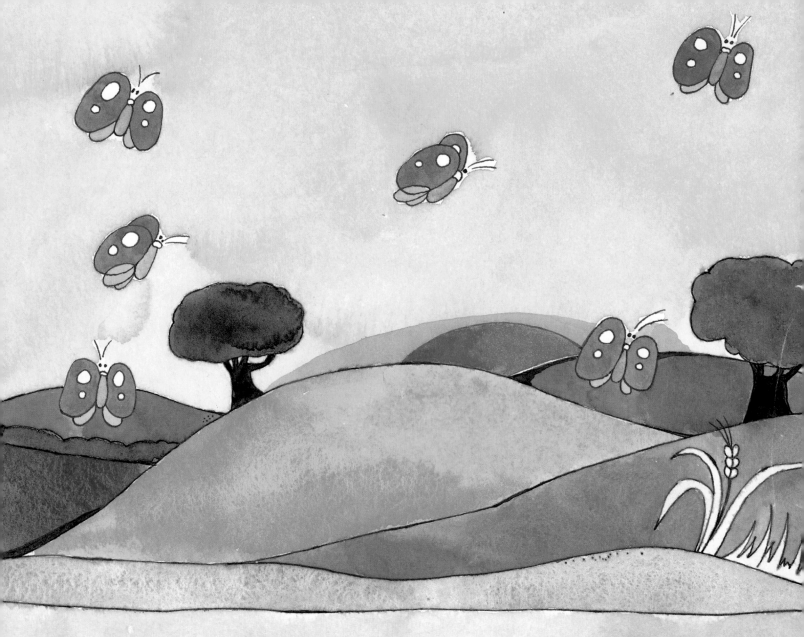

"Good!" said Mother.
"What can you count nine of?"

"I can count nine black ants,"
said Willy.
"Good!" said Mother.
"What can you count ten of?"

"I can count ten white sheep,"
 said Willy.
"Good!" said Mother.
"Now, what can you count one of?"

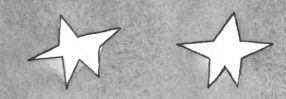

"One Daddy!" said Willy.
Then the three of them,
and one little dog,
and ten white sheep
walked all the way home together.